AF408267

Going to the Border

Vaya con Dios

Going to the Border

Vaya con Dios

By Judy Predmore

"We are a country where people of all backgrounds, all nations of origin, all languages, all religions, all races, can make a home. America was built by immigrants".

Hillary Clinton, former Secretary of State

Foreword

In October 2019, I volunteered for a month at Annunciation House in El Paso, Texas, a welcoming center ten miles from the Mexican border for people immigrating to the United States. I kept a daily journal and my plan was to come back and put my observations and reflections into a memoir reporting what I had seen and experienced. But I have struggled with how to tell this story. "Immigration" is such a controversial issue in our country right now. There have been conflicting views on what is really happening, what should be done, whether or not to build a wall, or whether to keep the borders open. I don't have answers to many of these questions. So, I kept putting the writing off.

As a retired high school ESL teacher-- ESL stands for "English as a Second Language"--, I used to teach teen immigrants and refugees from all around the world. One of my former students introduced me to his friend, Pedro, who wanted to tell his story about his journey to the United States from Guatemala. He knew I had written a book and wondered if I could write his story. He said his English was not very good, but he wanted others to know what he went through to get to the United States and why he made the dangerous journey. I told him I would help and then I realized I had the opportunity, not only to tell his story, but to incorporate my experiences too. So, this book looks at the issue of immigration from two very different perspectives. One is from Pedro. A teenage migrant traveling from Guatemala to the U.S. Southern border. The other is from me, a white, retired teacher from Western New York, who met and heard a number of stories from migrants during my month volunteering in El Paso, Texas.

I have tried to avoid the politics of a decades-long controversial issue and instead, I have focused on the humanitarian angle. The stories in the pages to follow are all true and as accurate as I can be. On occasion the names, like Pedro's, and places have been changed to protect the identities of the people involved.

To write this book I spent about three hours interviewing Pedro about his life, the timeline of his travels, and what he is doing now. Although Pedro could not always give me exact dates or names of places, his memories were vivid and he was quite honest and open about his life as a child, a traveling teen and now as a young adult of 21. He told me he wants people to hear his story and understand what he went through and why he made the decision to come to America.

I tried to capture Pedro's "voice" and mood with some exact quotes, but often I had to try to imagine and describe events and circumstances that I had not personally experienced. The stories I heard from others at the border were not as detailed or impassioned as what Pedro was able to share. He spoke from his heart and I was amazed by his inner strength, determination and resiliency in what he faced and was willing to share.

No matter where you stand on the issue of immigration today, we all must acknowledge immigration has been part of our country's history. For that reason, I believe it is important these stories continue to be told. Some may argue that today we are letting too many refugees into our country. Others will claim such actions are simply the humanitarian response. Either way, this book will report what I saw firsthand and how one young teen lived it. My hope is that my story and Pedro's story "going to the border" will help others develop a more informed opinion about immigration.

**The subtitle of this book, "Vaya Con Dios" translates from Spanish as "Go with God". Adios is the most common farewell message, but "Vaya con Dios" is normally used in religious contexts such as when saying goodbye to someone who is about to go on a long, dangerous journey.

"More than any other nation on earth, America has drawn strength and spirit from wave after wave of immigrants. In each generation, they have proved to be the most restless, the most adventurous, the most innovative, the most industrious of people. Bearing different memories, honoring different heritages, they have strengthened our economy, enriched our culture, renewed our promise of freedom and opportunity for all...."

President Bill Clinton

Background Information

Every day, all over the world, people make one of the most difficult decisions in their lives: to leave their homes in search of a safer, better life. Many people in the United States have had the experience of leaving the place where they grew up. Maybe they stay in the same area, the same village or city. Others move to another state, or across the country. But even then, returning "home" is common even if just to visit. But for those living in places fraught with war, famine or extreme poverty, they need is to leave their country behind, sometimes temporarily, but sometimes forever.

There are so many reasons why people around the globe rebuild their lives in a different country. Some may be pursuing their education or starting a new job. Some are forced to flee persecution or human rights violations. Millions flee from armed conflicts or other crises or violence. Still others are forced to move because they no longer feel safe and might be targeted for who they are or what they do or believe. This could be related to ethnicity, religious beliefs, sexual orientation or political views.

These journeys can also be full of danger and fear. Some risk falling prey to human trafficking and other forms of exploitation. Some are detained by the authorities as soon as they arrive in a new country. And still others, once they have settled into their new environment and are starting a new life, may face constant racism or discrimination. There may be feelings of loneliness or isolation because they have lost the support networks that most of us take for granted.

The terms "refugee" and "asylum seeker" are used to describe people who are on the move, who have left their country and crossed borders. There is an important distinction between these terms and legal differences as well.

According to the Amnesty International website, a refugee "is a person who has fled their own country because they are at risk of serious human rights violations and persecution there. The risks to their safety and life were so great that they felt they had no choice but to leave and seek safety outside their country because their own government cannot or will not protect them from those dangers." Usually, refugees have very little time to plan their journey, their situation changes quickly, they are in sudden danger, and they leave their homes with whatever they can carry. Sometimes families travel for days, weeks or months looking for refuge. And every year, hundreds of people die while trying to find refuge.

Refugees have a right to international protection. In 1980 President Jimmy Carter signed the Refugee Act into law. This established the Federal Refugee Resettlement Program to help refugees achieve economic self-sufficiency as quickly as possible after arrival into the United States. In the past several years we have seen refugees fleeing from Syria, many African nations, Iraq and Afghanistan during war times. Most recently, with the Russian attacks on Ukraine, there has been a sharp increase in Ukrainian refugees.

The United Nations High Commissioner for Refugees (UNHCR) states when refugees leave their home looking for safety, they become "asylum-seekers". In our country, an asylum seeker must pass background checks and health checks, in addition to answering many questions to prove who they are. This is known as vetting. Then they can be legally labeled a refugee. People who have committed crimes are not eligible for refugee status. Seeking asylum is a human right. The people entering the United States at the Southern border are asking for asylum and are screened by Border Patrol and must pass a "Credible Fear Interview" to be granted asylum in the United States. They still must report to Immigration Court for further processing of their claim and permission to remain in the country as a refugee. Refugees can apply for naturalization five years after admission to lawful permanent residence.

Although we have these terms and definitions, they simply describe the circumstances under which someone leaves his/her native country and what is needed to be allowed into ours. But none of these words encapsulate identity of the men, women, and children who have left their homes behind to start a new life in another country. These people are all unique human beings who have worth. They are grandparents, parents, children and siblings. Many are accomplished teachers, doctors, farmers, or artists. Their story is so much more than the unbearable circumstances from where they once lived.

In the United States, when a person under the age of 18 is not accompanied by a parent or legal guardian and is apprehended by immigration authorities, that person is transferred to the care and custody of the Office of Refugee Resettlement (ORR). Federal law requires that ORR feed, shelter and provide medical care for unaccompanied children until they are able to release them to safe settings with sponsors, either family members or organizations, while they await their immigration proceedings.

All sponsors of these children are required to pass a background check. The sponsor must agree to ensure the child's presence at all future immigration proceedings while providing a safe environment caring for their physical and mental well-being. In my area in Western New York, Catholic Family Services sponsors some of these children and they are placed in foster homes and enrolled in public schools.

We all want to live in a world where people who are in grave danger have the opportunity to build their lives in safety. Host communities benefit from the tremendous energy and drive to start new lives. They make the community more diverse and bring talents and gifts to their new home.

Most religions and cultural beliefs have some form of the Golden Rule which reinforces the humanitarian need to treat others with respect. They are:

Buddhism

Hurt not others with what which pains itself.

Christianity

Do unto others as you would have them do unto you.

Hinduism

Treat others as you would yourself be treated.

Islam

Do unto all men as you would wish to have done unto you.

Judaism

What you yourself hate, do to no man.

Native American

Live in harmony, for we are all related.

Sacred Earth

Do as you will, as long as you harm no one.

One argument against bringing more people into this country is that we should be taking care of our own first. There are a number of Americans living in poverty that could use help. Many are veterans that have served our country selflessly. That is very true and it is a tragedy. But we are one of the richest countries on the planet with more resources here than anywhere else. The poor, destitute of our nation are "wealthy" compared to the lives of the incoming refugees. How many times have you driven down the street and seen people throwing out "garbage" which is still usable? How many restaurants, stores, or even in our own homes, do we toss out perfectly good food which is still edible? We waste so many of our resources in this country.

It is important to know that the incoming migrants are not able to access welfare or food stamps. They are so grateful and appreciative to be in a safe place with freedom and a public education system. They will do work that not many Americans want to do. They work as janitors or custodians, Certified Nurse Assistants, food service and, agricultural workers. Some of my former students' parents with college degrees worked overnight shifts at Krispy Kreme donuts or were orderlies in hospitals, even though they had college degrees or were in prestigious jobs in their home countries. They are willing to do anything to survive and are so grateful to be in America.

Our country established a human value to treat all people with dignity. The Revolutionary War was fought for our freedom and independence. The newly formed government created a document stating that all are created equal. The Civil War was fought giving equality to African Americans. The 19th amendment gave women the right to vote and more equality.

Our country has always had the values to promise a safe harbor for people who are trying to start a better life or are fleeing persecution. One of our nation's symbols, the Statue of Liberty, was placed at Ellis Island welcoming many of our ancestors to this country. And Jimmy Carter's Refugee Act of 1980 drew nearly unanimous support when it was first established by Congress to welcome people who are fleeing from danger to this country. The United States has always been known for its compassion to others in need. It is one of our most fundamental values and we should be proud of that.

"When you get to know a lot of people, you make a great discovery. You find that no one group has a monopoly on looks, brains, goodness or anything else. It takes all the people— black and white, Catholic, Jewish, Protestant, Muslim, recent immigrants and Mayflower descendants—to make up America."

Judy Garland, Hollywood actress

JUDY

Why I Chose to Go to the Border

I grew up in a rural suburb of Rochester in New York on a 56 acre farm. I come from a loving family of six, two parents and three brothers and myself. I would say we were a middle-class family. I attended public school and never once did I have to worry about my safety or where my next meal was coming from. I lived a very comfortable life, felt loved and was living in a country where we celebrated our freedom and there were resources for those less fortunate. I was truly blessed.

I went to college and worked in the mental health field for 17 years then returned to college at the age of 40 to get my Masters in Teaching English to Speakers of Other Languages (TESOL). I then worked as an English as a Second Language (ESL) teacher for twenty years in a suburban high school in Western New York.

It was during my ESL career that I became more aware of global issues and seeing the world from different perspectives. For example, some of the Sophomore students I was working with were reading <u>Night</u> by Elie Wiesel in their English class. This book is a memoir of a Jewish man who lived during the World War II era and experienced the Holocaust. He described how his family was first moved to the Jewish ghettos, were then separated by gender, and eventually put on trains which took them to concentration camps. During one of the class discussions about this novel, one of my students asked me, "What would you have done if you lived during that time?" This led to a spirited discussion about whether we would have followed Hitler's dictates to remove the Jews into Ghettos, separate families, brand them with tattoos, pull the lever in the gas chamber and so forth? Or would we help to hide our neighbors in our basements and attics, lie to authorities and risk our own lives trying to help them escape? A third option would be to stand by quietly and let all this happen before our eyes. That classroom discussion has always stayed with me.

In 2015, a Syrian refugee crisis was broadcast every night on the news. Tens of thousands of Syrians were immigrating to Europe to avoid war and persecution. I witnessed the devastation and tragedies that were happening and wanted so badly to go and help out in some way. But I didn't because of my career and following my own personal adult responsibilities like paying the mortgage and other bills. More than once I asked myself if I was just "standing by" while this human tragedy was playing out?

As I was approaching retirement in June 2019, the news was hitting closer to home about the incoming migrants at the Southern border. I saw news reports about the separation of family members, people in cages and others dying as they tried to enter the country. My former student's question kept popping into my head, "what would you have done if you lived during that time?" I realized I was now living during "that time," or at least a time when others needed help. With my upcoming retirement perhaps now I would have the opportunity to do something more in a tangible way. So, I started exploring options online and praying for direction on what I could do.

One Sunday after church services, there was a presentation given by a religious woman who had volunteered at a place called Annunciation House in El Paso, Texas. This facility is a welcoming center for incoming refugees. I attended the talk and my heart began stirring as I realized that I had found an answer to my prayers. I spoke to her after the presentation and asked if it was safe for me to travel there alone to volunteer. She assured me it was and I started my online application to volunteer for a month after my retirement.

I retired in June 2019 and made a commitment to volunteer at Annunciation House the month of October that same year. Now I must admit that I was very selective in my choice of time. I googled the temperatures in El Paso, Texas and saw how hot it gets during the summer months. I don't do well with hot weather. The daytime temperatures were often over 100 degrees and only cooled down a little at night. In October the forecast predicted temperatures in the mid to high 80s and that was more bearable for me. A person of "white privilege" has the luxury to make this choice.

I also had the privilege and luxury to arrange my travel plans, which suited my schedule and rearrange other conveniences we take for granted so I could make this trip. For example, I put a hold on my mail and made sure my bills would be paid on time. I took my time packing for my trip and made sure I had what I needed for my month-long stay. As I was packing and trying to fit everything into a large suitcase, I kept thinking that it was impossible for me to get everything into the one suitcase. Since I knew I would have laundry services at the place I was staying so I decided to have enough clothes for one week. I also had my toiletries, books to read, my I pad and a journal.

As I worried about whether my one large suitcase would be sufficient to pack what I "needed" for my month long trip, a suitcase that I would check in at the airport and retrieve when I arrived in El Paso, it occurred to me that migrants I was about to meet had to pack everything they could take into a small backpack or suitcase which they would have to carry, for days or weeks across very long distances under very difficult circumstances. It also dawned on me that I was coming back to my home in a month. The people that I was about to meet started their journeys knowing that they would never return to their home. Quite a difference.

The day before I left for the border, I got an e-mail from the Volunteer Coordinator with my final instructions. She gave me the address of the facility where I would be living for the next month. It was in an industrial section of the city and there was no sign on the building. It was an old electric warehouse that was being renovated as a hospitality center. I would be given a bed in a dorm-like setting that used to house offices. I also was informed that I would be using a port-a-potty since there was limited indoor plumbing. I was assured there were indoor showers. There would be no Wi-fi in the building. All of this made me a little nervous, but again I thought about the luxuries I have enjoyed in my lifetime and I figured I could survive for a month with these challenges. I was most worried about going outside in the middle of the night to use the bathroom.

So, the next day I arrived at the airport at 6:15 AM and began my journey from Rochester, New York to El Paso, Texas. There was a three hour time difference and I arrived in El Paso it was 12:15. PM (really 3:15 PM Eastern Standard Time). I traveled 2,026 miles in about nine hours.

I checked my suitcase in Rochester and didn't have to carry it through the airport or when I transferred flights. My suitcase was waiting for me in baggage claim when I arrived in El Paso. During my flights I had a slightly cramped, but comfortable seat with access to a bathroom anytime I needed it. I was served drinks, snacks and a lunch on the plane and I had my cell phone with me at all times. I arrived to my final destination tired, but excited about my upcoming experience. Again, very different from what the migrants experienced in their travels.

"Nearly all Americans have ancestors who braved the oceans—liberty-loving risk takers in search of an ideal—the largest voluntary migrations in recorded history. Immigration is not just a link to America's past, it's also a bridge to America's future."

President George H. W. Bush

PEDRO

Why I Chose to Go to the Border

I grew up in Yalambojoch, a small village in Guatemala. I lived near the city of Huehuetenango. I don't have a lot of early memories of my parents. I just knew they were never around and I was on my own since about age 6 or 7. As I grew older, I realized my parents were both druggies and I had been abandoned. I never really learned what happened to my father, but my mother was always drunk or high and was not interested in taking care of me.

For most of my childhood during the day I would wander around the village and go off to play with friends by the river. We would swim and I had a carefree life, not worrying about much. We would catch little fish with our hands and then build a fire and boil them in water to eat them when we were hungry. Most of these friends would return to their homes when it got dark, but I didn't have a home to go to. So, I often slept on the ground under the stars or would sneak up onto someone's porch and sleep until the morning. When I was hungry, I had to climb a tree to pick some fruit or beg for food. Sometimes my friends would bring me something to eat from their homes.

I never went to school because in Guatemala you had to pay tuition and I didn't have any money nor a family to pay. So, when some of the kids were in school, I would walk around the village and do some work for people to get food. One nice storeowner befriended me when I was about 10 years old and he would let me work for him and in exchange he would give me food. I would sweep his front steps or take some food or candy and walk around the village selling his goods and then bring the money back to him. He then gave me some candy or chips to eat.

When I was about 8 years old, I met an older kid named Cesar who was about 4 years older than me. Cesar had the "mind of a child" and we became friends. We stayed together a lot and he watched over me and I watched over him. If kids started to tease or bully Cesar, I would step in and tell them to stop. Sometimes I wished to have a family and a home, but I always felt lucky to have my friend, Cesar and he became my family.

When I was about 11 years old, I started working on my own. I grew beans and corn to sell to people. That's how I survived. In the village of Guatemala where I lived, people didn't really own the land, but everyone could grow food. I just picked some land and got some seeds from the nice storeowner and started my business. It was a hard life but I never really knew any other way of living.

When I was about 12 years old, my uncle returned from Mexico. He was my father's brother and when he saw me and found out I had been living on the streets all these years, he offered to take me in. He felt bad that my father had deserted me and when I asked him about my father, my uncle just said, "it's better you don't know." I asked him how old I was and if he knew what year I was born. He found an old paper maybe my birth certificate that had my parents' names and the date I was born. I learned that I was born on May 4, 2002 and that I was now 12.

I moved in with my uncle and his wife. They had two older children but I didn't see them much. My uncle took care of me and fed me. He told me that I had to follow his rules and he sent me to school. I went for about a month but I was really far behind and it was too expensive. My uncle then told me that he needed more money and that I could work for him. So I did. I started as a delivery person but after a while I started drug smuggling. I would deliver cocaine and marijuana to people and then bring the money back to my uncle. The money was good, but it all went back to my uncle. I saw a lot of bad things at this time of my life and I felt unsafe. I always tried to be very careful but sometimes I would get beaten up and a few times men tried to have sex with me. I fought them off and ran away. I saw some boys my age being lured into the drug world and I was afraid that I would be next. I didn't want to live this kind of life but I didn't know what to do.

I started hearing stories or meeting people who had returned from the United States. They told me how they had gone up North for work and had sent money back to their family. I also heard some boys a little older than me were leaving Guatemala to go North to the States. They wanted to have a better life and I started thinking about that and if it would be possible for me. There were ads on the radio from people called "coyotes" who offered to help people travel North. This made me think it might be possible for me to actually do this.

I kept working for my uncle. Some of the loads that I carried were very heavy and my arms and legs would hurt so much. I needed to stop and rest. Most days I would arrive home around midnight and my uncle was drunk or relaxing at home. I was doing all the work and being put in danger and this was making me mad. At age 14 I had a fight with my uncle. I told him I wanted half of the money for the work I was doing. He didn't like that idea but I told him I wouldn't work for him anymore, so he finally agreed. That was when I started saving money. My uncle would try to take my money but I hid it well. Sometimes I put it inside my shoes or other secret places that he never found.

After about 18 months, I had saved up about $4,000 dollars in Guatemala money (quetzals) that would be worth about $12,000 in Mexican pesos. $1,000 quetzals equals about $127 U.S. dollars I thought that was enough to travel North. I started talking to more and more people about my plan. I met a coyote that others said was good and he told me to buy a pair of good hiking boots for the journey. He told me not to bring any documents or ID with me. That was good because I didn't have anything except that old paper that my uncle had with my birthdate.

I started saying goodbye to my friends. Cesar, my best friend, begged me to stay. He said he would be all alone. I told him I had to go; I couldn't keep living like this anymore. I've got to have a better life. He asked me if he could go along with me but I didn't have enough money saved for both of us. I promised him that when I made it to the United States, I would start sending him money so he could come up to live with me in the States. We both cried when I said goodbye to him. I went to find my mother who had remarried and had more children. I told her my plan and she didn't seem to care at all. I told her I would never contact her again and walked away. I said goodbye to my uncle who had taken care of me for a number of years and his new son who was now 3 years old. I was 15 years old and ready to start the next phase of my life.

"Give me your tired, your poor, your huddled masses yearning to breathe free. The wretched refuse of your teeming shore. Send these, the homeless, tempest-tossed, to me: I lift my lamp beside the golden door."

Emma Lazarus, quote on the Statue of Liberty at Ellis Island

Judy

Arrival to Annunciation House

I arrived in El Paso, Texas at 12:15 PM. I summoned a taxi at the airport and as instructed by the e-mail contact from Annunciation House, I gave the address to a local restaurant near the building where I would be housed. There would be no sign on the door of where I would be staying. Homeland Security had requested all signage to be taken down to keep the building as private and secure as possible from possible protesters or violent attacks.

Two months prior to my arrival in El Paso, there had been a mass shooting at a Walmart Shopping Plaza about 10 minutes away from where I was to stay. A twenty-one year old man filled with hatred targeted and killed 23 people, and injured 22 more. This domestic terrorist attack was described as the deadliest attack on Latinos in modern American history. (I visited the site during my stay and saw see the memorials of flowers, photos and mementos of the people that had died.)

On the way to the facility, I talked with the taxi driver about my volunteer plans and he shared with me that he had worked at a detention center for unaccompanied minors for two years and was so grateful that I was coming down from New York to help out. He also warned me that I would be hearing some harrowing stories and may feel overwhelmed. I told him I was ready. I thought I was at least.

We got to the address of the restaurant I had given and then I told him to drive past to the large unmarked building and leave me at the blue awning with stairs where I was told to ring the doorbell for entrance. I arrived about 1:15 PM.

I quickly learned this place was called the Casa del Refugiado (Refugee House) and was only one of the sites of Annunciation House. Ruben Garcia is currently the Executive Director of this non-profit founded back in 1978 to aid immigrants fleeing violence in Central America and Mexico. This facility where I was assigned was set up in April 2019 to provide immediate assistance to those seeking asylum, most of whom do not speak English and have only a sketchy knowledge of the size of the United States, the location of their sponsor here, or how they were supposed to meet up with their sponsor. This building used to be an electrical supplies warehouse and was being converted to house up to 1,000 guests if needed. One of the volunteers let me in and guided me through several hallways to the Main Office where I was greeted by the Lead Volunteer. I was early for my 2:00 orientation so she directed me to sit in the office to relax and watch for a while.

There was a hustle and bustle all around me as the volunteers came in and out of the office and answered three phones ringing. Most of the volunteers spoke fluent Spanish and I immediately thought to myself that I was ill prepared. I only had basic conversational Spanish, not enough to answer and converse with someone over the phone. There were several bulletin boards around the room with small post-it notes of guests and their travel plans. In between the phone calls, some of the volunteers started to explain procedures to me but we were often interrupted by business.

My orientation began at 2:00, but within a half hour we had to stop as a Border Patrol bus pulled up bringing 35 new arrivals. My orientation became a "hands on" learning as I was paired up with one of the more seasoned volunteers and told to work in the Hygiene Room. I was able to observe the "guests" being welcomed and brought to a large area with chairs and tables where volunteers started the Intake process which consisted of asking each family who they were traveling with and contact information about their Sponsors. Most of the new arrivals were clutching a piece of paper with a name and phone number scrawled onto it with the name and phone number of a relative or friend who had agreed to take responsibility for them. I could see they guarded that piece of paper as though their life depended on it, and in many cases, it did. I noticed some young children had the phone number of their Sponsor written on their skin with permanent marker. The Shift Coordinator explained to me this was done in case they get separated from their family. The person doing the interview took the information on the paper (or the child's skin) and contacted the Sponsor to start the process.

Each guest was wearing an ID bracelet similar to what you would wear in the hospital as their identification from one of detention centers. We would cut these bracelets off their wrists and tell them they were now free. One person from each family also wore an ankle monitor on and I thought to myself that is what they put on prisoners who are on House Arrest. I learned that they had been granted temporary asylum and would keep that ankle bracelet on until they went to their first immigration court proceeding in the location they were traveling to. It still bothered me to see them forced to wear these like they were a criminal.

Each guest was given a bottle of water and granola bar and told to keep the water bottle to be refilled throughout their stay. When they finished with the initial data collection, the new arrivals were sent to the Hygiene Room and given a clean towel, various hygiene products. (toothbrush and paste, comb, deodorant, feminine hygiene products, razors and diapers, if needed), and a blanket and sheets for their cots which had been provided by the American Red Cross. With my limited Spanish and a lot of pointing, I was able to communicate at a very basic level with the guests. Right away

I observed a mix of reactions. Some people had a blank affect, almost like they were in a trance, no doubt from the uncertainty they had faced. Most were holding hands or standing very close to their family members, looking disheveled and exhausted from their long bus ride. Amazingly, others had big smiles and kept saying "gracias" for all that they were given.

I asked one young mother who was holding a 6 to 8 month old baby how many diapers she needed. She replied "one". I handed her about six and told her that she could get more from us if she needed. She said in the detention center where she had come from that they were only granted one diaper per day. I asked the children what color towel they wanted and they seem surprised that they were given a choice. Their parent usually smiled down at them and nodded that they could select their own color. We also gave out new shoelaces because the detention centers would confiscate them from their shoes. (I guess they worry about suicides) I learned later in my stay that the detention centers also confiscated medicines like insulin or high blood pressure pills which were not returned upon their release.

After these new arrivals had gone through the Hygiene Room, another volunteer came and escorted them to the Sleeping Quarters, El Dormitorio, where they were assigned cots. When these new arrivals had been situated, I thought my Orientation would resume. Instead, a group of about thirty guests were soon to go to the bus station and they needed to have a meal before their departure. I was then assigned to another volunteer to help set up leftover food from a previous meal in the dining area for them. I never did finish my orientation.

The regular dinner was provided that evening at 6:00 PM by a local church group. I learned that this group came in every Wednesday to prepare and serve the meal. I sat at a table with other volunteers and began to hear their stories of where they were from and their time commitments.

I learned that first day that this site of Annunciation House is a Hospitality Center that welcomes the migrants after being processed by Border Patrol. The migrants come from several local detention centers in the El Paso area. Annunciation House is run by all volunteers. Some come for two weeks, others like me make a month-long commitment and still others dedicate a full year to volunteer in this place with a meager stipend. Some of the volunteers I met were former Peace Corp volunteers, others were young adults who had just graduated from college, and several retired people, like me. There were a few who had taken some time off from their daily jobs to come down on their vacation to work. There were a few from various religious orders too. We were from all over the United States. In addition, there were some El Paso community members who volunteer once a week to help out. There were a mixture of ages and occupations. But we were all there with the same purpose, to welcome the migrants into our country.

Right from the start I was amazed at the process and coordination I was observing. And within minutes of arrival, the guests were beginning to feel the sense of welcome and compassion given to them at this place. I feel like we are honoring the quote from the Statue of Liberty at Ellis Island. (Give me your tired, your poor…)

I was finally shown my room about 8:00 PM and I was exhausted. I found out that I was rooming with two young women in their twenties. I had a single bed and was shown where the sheets and blankets were kept. I began making my bed and settling my personal belongings. I took time to write a reflection in my daily journal and post a message on Facebook. I was in bed by about 9:30 PM. Thoughts of the day flooded my mind but because I was dealing with a three hour time difference, I fell asleep rather quickly. I was thankful I wasn't assigned to work an eight hour shift until 2:00 PM the next day. That would give me the morning to get more acclimated, take a shower and settle into my temporary home.

"A child on the other side of the border is no less worthy of love and compassion than my own child."

President Barack Obama

Pedro

My Journey Begins

I got up early the day I was leaving and walked for about four or five hours to the bus station where I would meet the coyote. There were about 20 others who were traveling with him. He planned to put us all on a bus that headed North to the border of Guatemala and Mexico. He showed us a map and the plans for our journey. Sometimes we would ride in a bus or truck, sometimes we would walk and part of the trip would be on a train. He wasn't going to stay with us all the time. He said he would meet us next at the bus station near the Mexican border. I had to give the coyote $2,000 quetzals for his help and towards the bus ticket. I think the bus ticket was about $400 quetzals. The coyote told me to hide any money I had left, so I put it in my shoes.

I stood observing the others who were traveling in this caravan as we waited for the bus to arrive. There were some people traveling alone and some families with young kids. Many were from Guatemala and some were from Honduras and El Salvador. Everyone seemed to speak a different language and I only understood parts of what they were saying. I didn't know growing up that there were different languages and dialects. I came to learn that I spoke an indigenous Mayan dialect.

Some of the others were carrying backpacks and bags. I had a small sack with another shirt, a hoodie, a hat, my phone, some snacks that the nice store owner had given to me for the journey and a water bottle. I felt ready.

The bus arrived and we all boarded. I went towards the back of the bus and sat by the window. When it took off, I looked out the window for my final farewell to this place called home. I had no idea what lay ahead but I was excited to be going.

My eyes teared up as I thought about Cesar who I had to leave behind. I would miss him but for now I had to take care of myself. I watched as the bus left my village and all that I knew. The roads were bumpy and curvy and after about an hour I closed my eyes to rest up for the trip. I must have fallen asleep because when I opened them again the landscape looked very different. We were in a place that I had never seen before and the roads were even more bumpy.

The bus stopped along the way at other small villages and towns. Some people got off, but mostly more people got on the bus. The bus was slowly making its way up north to Mexico. The trip was about 8 hours long. When we got to the border of Mexico, our caravan got off the bus and we found our coyote. He showed us the map again and instructed us that we would be walking for about 2 or 3 hours to another village and he would meet us there. He told us to always look around to see if there were any police. He told us that if we did, we should run and try to hide. We didn't see anyone on this part of our journey.

We had to stop several times for breaks, for the young children or to find a private place to go to the bathroom. The coyote was waiting for us at the next village and this time he had a large delivery truck. We all got in the back of the truck and sat down. It was about midnight and the coyote told us that we would be safer traveling at night. He said we should try to sleep if we could because the next part of the journey would be hard. I can't remember the names of the places that we stopped, I just put all my trust in this coyote to keep me safe and get me to the border. I did get some sleep even though the ride was very bumpy. That night we made it to District Federal (near Mexico City).

Upon our arrival we had to walk for a few hours towards the train tracks. We were walking down a mostly empty road with no cars or people. I had no idea where we were. During our rest breaks, the coyote explained to us about riding the train. It was called "The Beast". We would be getting on at a place where the train tracks curve and the train slows down, but it wouldn't be stopping. We would have to run alongside the train and jump up and grab one of the ladders on the side. He said the train can "eat you alive" and that's why it's called The Beast. He explained that when you jump up to the ladder you must put your leg closer to the train up first and that you would have to be strong and pull yourself up before the train pulls you under it. He said to climb the ladder to the top of the train. He said when the train went through towns with lots of people, we should lay down flat so people wouldn't see us on top. I started to worry but I pushed down the fears and focused on my dream and my strength.

I could hear the train approaching in the distance. The coyote told us that all that made it onto the train should stay on top until it stops at another city. He would be waiting for us there. My heart started racing and I could feel the energy pumping in my body. One young man from Honduras started running alongside the train and I watched how he pulled himself up on the train. I was next and I did exactly what he did and I made it. I climbed to the top and looked back down to watch the others. The families with little kids were not going to try. A few others made it up to the top but about half of our group didn't. I think the coyote was giving them directions on where to walk and I never saw any of them again.

The train started moving faster after it went around the curve and I had to find a safe place to sit. I didn't want to fall off the side. I knew I had to stay awake during this part of the journey. There were small groups of people all over the top of the train and many looked dusty, dirty, and tired.

I thought to myself that I probably looked the same. I tried to ignore my hunger pain. I started to have pains in my back, my legs, my feet. I also had pain in my heart as I left behind everything I had known. This may have been the greatest pain, but I tried to focus on my future and what lays ahead for a better life.

We stayed on the train for about 4 or 5 hours before it stopped and we got down and started looking for our coyote. When we met him, we walked us to a quiet place where we could sleep for a few hours before the next part of our journey where we would be walking for a while. He gave each of us a new water bottle and a snack before we went to sleep. Again, he said it would be safer to travel at night. I tried to sleep as close to the coyote as I could because if I didn't wake up in time, I would be lost and I had no idea which way to go. I didn't want to get separated from him. We all slept about four or five hours. Our group which started out with twenty people was now down to about seven.

We started walking in the late evening. I tried to walk close to the coyote. If he ran, I would run. I didn't want to get separated from him. But after about an hour the coyote saw the police coming and he told us to run. But the police were too fast and they caught us. The coyote vanished and the police searched our bodies and took all of my money and my phone. They said we had to go back to our countries and they brought us to different jails. Me and an older Guatemalan man went to one jail where we stayed for a couple of weeks. Then the police brought us to a bus station and gave us a ticket to return to Guatemala. I never got my money back or my phone.

I was so sad. I had gone so far and now had to return to my village with my head down. But I was not yet ready to give up.

"People will forget what you said. People may forget what you did. But people will never forget how you made them feel."

Maya Angelou, poet

Judy

Day 2 at Annunciation House

I slept in until about 9 AM. I did have to get up in the middle of the night and went outside to use the port-a-potty. I brought along my I phone to use as a flashlight because it was dark in the hallways and outside. I was worried I would drop the phone into the latrine.

In the morning, I went into the Volunteer Lounge and poured myself a cup of coffee and looked on the snack shelf for something to eat. There was a loaf of bread and some peanut butter so I made myself some toast. There was a bowl of fruit and I helped myself to a banana. While I was eating, two volunteers came in and introduced themselves to me and we chatted. I told them this was my first official day and I planned to take a shower and get more acclimated before my 2 PM shift. One offered to show me where the showers were when I was ready. I went to my room and got my stuff and she walked me to the showers. It was quite a walk and I laughed and said I hope that I could find my way back. There were 2 bathrooms, one for men and one for women, but the toilets were not functional. I took my shower and then got dressed there before returning to my room. I did, in fact, get lost on my way back to my room. I felt like I had walked a half mile there and half mile back.

It was now about 10:30 AM and I had a chance to chat with one of my roommates who had a day off. She and two other young ladies were planning to go out shopping and for lunch somewhere in El Paso. They told me there were quite a few volunteers leaving on Saturday but that a new batch would be coming in to replace them.

I walked down to the office about 11:45 AM because I knew that lunch was being served at noon. I met a few more volunteers and they walked me down to the dining area for lunch. Today another community group brought in rice and beans, brisket, tortilla chips and shells, tomatoes and lettuce. The food was delicious and I sat with the volunteers again and just observed everything for a while.

I noticed that some volunteers sat with families and I thought to myself, "I would like to do that too." Even though I had limited Spanish, I wanted to intermingle and thought I would do that at dinner. I noticed that young, single mothers who had babies or toddlers were often helped by others. One young child in a highchair was fussing and a little girl of about five years old from another family, got up and went over to the baby and tried to distract her so that her mother could eat. Some of these families had traveled together but many of them met at the detention center or here at Annunciation House. They bonded together because they had all shared similar experiences.

I was impressed by how the guests took part in cleaning up the dining area at the end of the meal. The volunteers came out with push brooms and several men jumped up to take them and sweep. The kids ran over to get the cleaning spray bottles and helped wipe down the tables. Everyone that could, placed their chairs up on top of the table after they were cleaned and the trash was placed in the large waste baskets. Again, some men helped to pull out the full bags and took them outside to the dumpsters. I asked one of the seasoned volunteers if they had been assigned these duties and he responded that "no, they just all are so grateful for being in a safe place and want to help."

After lunch I returned to my room at about 1 PM and rested on my bed before my shift. I checked e-mails and Facebook messages and was excited to learn more about this program. There was a brief meeting at

2:00 PM with all the evening volunteers and jobs were assigned. I started off in the Playroom and was told there always needed to be two adults in the room. Over the three hours that I was there I met about thirty children and some parents who accompanied them.

The room was filled with a variety of toys, stuffed animals, picture books and tables with art materials or a place to play games. This was my chance to try out some of my Spanish because I felt so much safer talking to children. I started with four young boys about age 10 and we played Pick Up Sticks. Once they understood the game, they became quite good and we had a lot of fun and laughter. All during that time I was also watching the younger kids with the toy trucks, blocks or dolls on the floor. Some played alone while others interacted with one another. There were a few who just sat passively on the floor and may have been overwhelmed with all the colors and excitement around them. Or maybe they had never had toys before.

A young father chose a coloring book and was helping his two kids start to color. I told him that he could color too and he smiled and chose a picture. I could almost see the tension melt from his face as he colored his picture. We hung up their pictures on the wall with tape and the father thanked me for what I was doing.

One young boy who was about 12 years old sat all alone with paper and markers. I went over to check in on him and I noticed that his drawing was very dark with some disturbing images. I smiled at him and sat down with some paper to color with him but we didn't talk. After a few minutes I noticed he grabbed some colors and added a rainbow to his drawing. Now, I am not an art therapist, but I could definitely interpret the meaning behind his drawing as an expression of all he had seen on his journey north and the fact that he added a rainbow in the corner may have been an indication of hope.

About 4:45 PM I tried to announce in Spanish that we needed to clean up and go back to get ready for dinner. About half of the kids looked at me with questioning looks and they either didn't understand my broken Spanish or they spoke an indigenous language. Thankfully, one of the parents in the room got up and repeated what I said and the kids all got up and helped put the toys away and returned to their parents back by their cots in the sleeping area before dinner.

When I got back to the office, I was instructed by the group leader to help escort about 45 guests outside to wait for the city bus that would be delivering some to the bus station and others to the airport. I went with a volunteer who was also a priest. He brought along a bottle of water and when we got outside, he gave a blessing to everyone and sprinkled water upon them. I was touched by this and saw how devoted everyone was and appreciated the final blessing on their journey. Several people came up to me and thanked me and gave me hugs, some that I had never met before. Two of the young boys that I had played Pick Up Sticks with in the Play Room came over and gave me a big hug. Their parents thanked me for all that I had done for their families. I continually said, "Vayan con Dios"…. go with God. There were a lot of smiles and some tears as we said our goodbyes.

One young mother with her three year old daughter was standing off to the side all alone. She had tears in her eyes. I went over and gave her a big hug but couldn't really give her any comforting words due to my limited Spanish. But that hug seemed to be enough for her and she held on tightly for about a minute before releasing me. I smiled at her, nodded and told her in English that everything would be okay. Then I said "Vaya con Dios".

I learned that night that the El Paso City Bus Transit Department donates buses to transport the migrants each day to the Greyhound Bus

Station and to the airport. While we were outside, a young man drove up with his wife and brought me two large bags of clothing that he was donating to the Center. I thanked him and asked how he knew about this place because I thought it was kept secret. He told me that his church brings meals during the week and although he can't help out with that, his family wanted to help out this way with donating clothing. I was amazed at how the El Paso community has stepped up to help in so many different ways.

I went back inside and was able to join the dinner meal late. I wasn't able to join any of the families because they were almost finished. Just when I was taking my final bites, the Lead Volunteer came over to me and said Border Patrol had just called and there was a new busload coming in. There were three families, about 14 people total. I was stationed in the Hygiene Room again after they had completed their Intake Interview. This time I worked alone. I had a pair of scissors and helped cut off their ID wrist bracelets from the Detention Center and we exclaimed "Libertad" in Spanish which means freedom.

As the families were settling their bedding in the sleeping area, the Lead Volunteer asked me to go down to the Ropa Room (clothing room). This was another new experience for me as I observed and helped out.

After the guests got their hygiene supplies and settled their beds, they were brought to the Ropa Room to select new outfits. The Ropa Room looks like a big thrift store. Now, I understood about the donated clothing that had been dropped off earlier. Volunteers work in this area to separate clothing by sizes and each guest is allowed to pick one new, gently used outfit. Each guest is also given brand new underwear, socks and some select shoes. After they leave the Ropa Room, they are allowed to take a shower in an outdoor mobile shower trailer that is hooked up for them. They now had a clean outfit to put on rather their dirty traveling clothes, which some have been wearing for days or weeks.

While the three new families were "shopping", I offered to hold a baby so that a young mother could go through the bins to find clothing for her three young children. She was hesitant at first but I just looked at her and smiled and I said "abuela" which is Spanish for grandmother. This convinced her and she handed me her little one. Her two other children stayed with me and their baby sister and I started singing children's songs to them. Wheels on the Bus, Twinkle, Twinkle Little Star, Old McDonald. I wished that I knew some Spanish children's songs but they seemed to enjoy listening and smiled. The mother kept looking over at me and smiling and she was able to get all her shopping done without interruption.

After the families had left, I asked the other volunteer where all the clothes had come from and she said they were mostly from donations. She said local schools and churches have done clothing drives for Annunciation House. Some of the guests take the new clothes and leave behind their clothing which gets washed in the laundry room if it is still in good condition. She also informed me that several volunteers leave behind their clothes to donate to the supply. And finally, some volunteers on their days off, go to local thrift shops to buy up clothing sizes that are needed. Later that evening I found out my roommate and her two friends had done just that. Again, I was amazed at the kindness before my eyes.

I couldn't believe it was already 9:30 PM and my shift was coming to an end. I went back to the office for my final check-in and then returned to my room to catch up on e-mails, write my daily Facebook message and wind down from the day.

"We are a nation of immigrants. We are the children and grandchildren of the ones who wanted a better life, the driven ones, the one who woke up at night hearing that voice telling them that life in that place called America could be better."

Senator Mitt Romney

Pedro

My Second Attempt

People were surprised to see me walk back into my village. I told them I had gotten caught by police and had to come back but that I wasn't giving up. I went to my uncle and begged him for money to try again. At first, he said "no". Then I pleaded and said if he didn't give me the money, I would kill myself and he would have to live the rest of his life with the guilt. He finally agreed to give me $1000 quetzals and an old phone. I contacted the same coyote and he told me he had a group leaving in two days. He told me to meet them at the same bus station as before.

I said my goodbyes again and left early in the morning to walk to that bus station four hours away. This time there were about 40 people traveling. Some more were from Honduras, El Salvador, Ecuador and about half from Guatemala. We waited for the bus and planned to get off again at the Guatemala Mexican border. I fell asleep because I knew there was a long journey ahead.

The bus did stop at several small towns and at one of these stops a policeman got on the bus and started shining a bright light into everyone's faces. He asked each person where they were from and I told him "Guatemala". He said I could stay on the bus. The people from the other countries had to get off the bus. I looked around and we had lost about half of our group. We continued on until we arrived at the Mexican border and saw our coyote waiting for us.

I talked to the coyote and told him I wanted to get a bus ticket to go

57

as far North as possible for $500 quetzals. I asked him to help me buy a ticket and find the right place to wait for the bus. Two other teens wanted to do the same thing and he helped us. I now only had $100 quetzals left and the coyote told me I could trade that money in Mexico and I would get about $300 pesos. The three of us got on the bus. The two others were friends so they sat together in the back of the bus. I sat by myself in another place on the bus. After about an hour or two, the bus was stopped by police in Mexico. The policeman walked around the bus and was asking people where they were from. The two other Guatemalans were questioned and they were kicked off the bus. I leaned my head against the window and pretended to be asleep. The policeman went past me and I was never questioned. When the policeman got off the bus, I said to myself that I was very lucky and that maybe God was watching over me.

I was on this bus from about 8:30 PM until 11 AM the next morning. I think I got off at Alamos, Mexico, but I don't really remember the names of all the places that I traveled. When I got off the bus, I was in a strange place and I wasn't really sure what to do next. My coyote had given me a contact for another coyote where I got off, but wasn't sure if I would be safe. I had heard stories about bad coyotes taking advantage of people and I had no idea where to go and couldn't really read the maps posted in the bus station. So, I sat on a bench in the bus station and just thought for a while. I finally got up my courage and texted the new coyote. He was expecting my call and he said he could help me get through the desert but that I would have to give him all the money I had left. I only had $300 pesos and he said he was helping me out because the other coyote told him I was a good kid. Again, I was grateful that I was getting help.

The new coyote told me he would be meeting a group of people coming in on the next bus about 2 PM and that I should wait around that area. He told me what he was wearing and I told him what I was wearing and when the next bus arrived, I saw him standing off to the side. I went over and introduced myself. The new bus travelers started coming over and there were a lot of different people of all ages and from many different countries. I think there were about seventeen of us.

We walked for about a half hour to a big building and were told to rest up for a day and get some food to eat before the next part of our journey. The coyote wanted us to drink a lot of water because when we started walking in the desert we would sweat and lose a lot of water from our bodies. He said we would be in the desert for about 3 days so we needed to be rested and ready.

This new group of people were very nice to me. I told them that this was my second time going North and I was all by myself. Several of them shared their food with me and I felt accepted into their group. But even so, I was very careful because I didn't trust anyone.

After eating and talking for a while I went to a quiet area and tried to sleep. I needed all of my strength for the desert. I thought a lot about my life at that moment; my parents, my uncle and his family, my friend Cesar and my grandmother. I remember she had told me stories about God when I was really little and she said he is everywhere you look….in the sun, in the moon, in the plants and inside of people. I didn't really understand all of this but she said if I ever felt alone or needed strength to ask God for help. I definitely needed his help now.

The coyote came back about 12 hours later and checked on all of us. He wanted everyone to eat more food and drink more water. He gave each of us a gallon jug with water and said we would have to carry it across the desert. We had to make it last for 3 days. We would be leaving that night at about 7 PM because it is cooler walking through the desert at night. Everyone ate, drank and got ready to go.

That night we started walking and the coyote kept telling us we had to stay together and not get too far behind. He told us if he blew a whistle that meant we were in danger of getting caught and we had to run as fast as we could and hide. This scared me a little and I tried to stay as close to the coyote as I could. I didn't want to lose him or get separated from the group.

As the sun was setting and night was starting, the temperature started to drop. I pulled out my hoodie from my sack and put it on. I couldn't stop very long because I didn't want to lose my place near the coyote. We walked and walked. The coyote kept yelling back to the stragglers that they had to keep up because we had a long way to go. The mothers and fathers took turns carrying the little ones who couldn't keep up. It got darker and darker. I asked the coyote how he knew which way to go and he said he watches the sky. He always puts the moon to the right side and he knows that he is going North.

We finally stopped to take a break after about 5 hours of walking. My feet hurt and I can feel blisters forming. The coyote reminds everyone to take sips of water but to not drink too much because we have to make the gallon of water last for 3 days. I can hear real coyotes crying out in the night and I am glad that I am with this group for protection.

After a break of about thirty minutes, we started walking again. Now it was very dark. Everything looks the same. It doesn't feel like we are going anywhere. It's the same shrubs and dirt and nothingness. We keep walking.

I start thinking about all that I have seen and done so far. The bus rides, the police, the truck ride, losing people along the way, the train ride, the hunger, the thirst, the pain. But I keep walking. I am getting very tired. My body is hurting. But I keep walking.

The sun starts to come up, but we keep walking. I take off my hoodie and put it back into my sack. The coyote says we will continue walking until the sun is above us in the sky and then we will rest. He knows of a place up ahead that has some shrubs and a cave in the side of the mountain where we can rest and sleep in the shade away from the hot sun. It is starting to get really hot, but I don't want to drink too much water because I don't want to run out. We keep walking.

We finally stop to rest. The coyote passes out some small snacks and tells everyone to sip some water and then to get some rest. I stay close by the coyote and I don't want to sleep so hard that I don't hear him and the others wake up and leave. I don't want to be alone here in the desert.

I sleep for about five hours. I wake up and the coyote is not near me and I start to panic. But then I see others and I know the group is still here. I get up and find a place to go to the bathroom. I see the coyote and go over to ask him when we will be leaving. He said it was still too hot, maybe another 2 or 3 hours because the sun was still too high in the sky. He told me to get more rest but I don't want to fall asleep and risk everyone leaving. So, I just go and sit under a shrub to get out of the sun.

The coyote starts walking around and waking up people a few hours later and tells them to get ready to leave in about thirty minutes. I drink a little more water and eat a snack from my sack. The sun has gone down lower in the sky and all of the sudden I hear the sound of a helicopter. The sound starts to get louder. The coyote blows his whistle and shouts "RUN!".

Everyone runs in different directions to hide. The helicopter gets closer and there is a large spotlight moving across the desert. Then I hear dogs barking in the distance. I start running as fast as I can to get away from the dogs. I don't want to get caught. I run and run and find a good place to hide. I am all by myself and my heart is racing. I wait quietly and the sounds of the dogs get further and further away from me. I don't hear the helicopter anymore. I think I was hiding for about an hour or more. I don't know, I don't have a watch and my phone doesn't work in the desert.

When it all seems quiet, I come out from my hiding place. It is now very dark. I call for the coyote but don't hear anything. I yell "Help" but no one responds. I am so scared. I think I am all alone. I keep calling for about thirty minutes and nobody answers me. I am in the middle of the desert all by myself and I don't know which way to go. I have been alone most of my life but I have never felt so alone as I do right now. I sit down in the dirt and start crying. What am I going to do now?

"I had always hoped that this land might become a safe and agreeable asylum to the virtuous and persecuted part of mankind, to whatever nation they might belong."

President George Washington

Judy

My Assignment

I was scheduled again for the 2:00 PM to 10:00 PM shift. I slept well the night before and did have to get up during the night to use the outdoor port-a-potty. It was raining and there was a big puddle out in the parking lot that I had to walk around to get there. This outdoor bathroom was making my volunteer placement more challenging but I just kept reminding myself that this is nothing compared to what the migrants must have been through on their journeys.

I had a leisurely breakfast in the Volunteer Lounge and chatted with a few more volunteers, I was finally remembering names. They explained that each Lead Volunteer runs their shifts a little differently so we needed to adjust to the various leadership styles and personalities. I went back to the room and caught up on e-mails and Facebook posts and actually got teary eyed reading the posts of encouragement from friends.

I was on my way out to the bathroom mid-morning and one of the Volunteer Coordinators and Shift Leaders stopped me and asked if we could talk. She had reviewed my application and saw my skill set and knew I would be there for a month. She said that since I had been a teacher, she knew I must be organized and could anticipate changes. She said she would like me to train to become the Travel Package Coordinator. She said I could train with the current leader who would be leaving in a few days. In this role, my primary responsibility would be to stay abreast of when new migrants arrive and when they are leaving. She said I would have less contact with the guests and more with staff who would be helping me. My

65

schedule would be 7:00 AM to 3:00 PM every day.

I felt honored that she thought I could handle this responsibility and I agreed to take on this assignment. With this change, my work schedule for the day was adjusted so I could start training with Lucas, a former Peace Corp volunteer from Canada. He gave me an overview of the program and started my orientation.

As Travel Package Coordinator every day I had to check the bulletin boards in the office for new arrivals and expected departures. Travel bags are prepared for families to take on the next part of their journey. They contained peanut butter sandwiches, chips, granola bars or other snacks, and bottled water. The tote bag also contained a tactfully worded English note stapled on the inside explaining that these are refugees that don't speak English and it was asking for help to navigate an airport or bus station. If there were young children in the family, they may also receive a small coloring book and crayons and a tiny stuffed animal. Diapers were included for those needing them.

Lucas had developed a well-organized system for departures. He had a color-coded map of the U.S. that depicted the destinations of each family or guest. He tracked who was in each family that included ages of children, where they were going and how they were traveling (bus or airplane). Those families that had longer travel experiences would receive more food and drink. Those taking a plane would receive less. Lucas explained there were three departures each day. The first was about 8:00 AM, another mid-day and the final departure was around 6:00 PM. I had to be sure the bags were packed and brought up to the office about half hour before departure.

Anticipating future arrivals was a bit more challenging. I had to be sure that there were sandwiches made and ready to be packed in case there were unexpected arrivals and departures outside of my shift. If food supplies like bread or bottled water got low, I had to notify the Shift Coordinator so that they could get more.

When new arrivals came, I would bring out a cart with bottled water and snacks to pass out while welcoming the guests to the facility. That cart had to be ready at all times because the arrivals were whenever Border Patrol showed up.

There was also a side room filled with diapers. Lucas showed me the changing station out in the warehouse and that he had to check each day and replenish with diapers and baby wipes when needed. Finally, there were big sports thermos containers in the hallways that had to be kept filled with water. The guests could refill their water bottles from these containers throughout their stay. I recalled watching one young boy of about five years old filling up his bottle with his father. He looked up at him when the water started flowing and smiled saying, "the water looks so clean!". It made me wonder what water he had been drinking all along his journey.

It seemed like a lot to do but Lucas reminded me volunteers are assigned to work with me and I would catch on quickly. He also mentioned there were always side projects to do. For example, we would create small travel packs of baby wipes for the travel bags that would be included when there were diapers. Another project was to package up formula baggies with instructions in Spanish.

I was excited to get started. And I must admit the nicest feature of this site was that it was in an air-conditioned area in order to keep the food fresh. Because of this a lot of volunteers stopped in throughout their shifts to cool off. The one downfall was that I would have less contact with the guests but I could still join them during the meals.

I worked with Lucas for 3 days to learn the ropes and then I took over. I can't believe that after just five days that I would be running such an important part of the program.

"Strength of character isn't always about how much you can handle before you break. It's about how much you can handle after you've been broken."

Robert Tew, author

Pedro

Alone in the Desert

I don't know how long I sat in the dirt crying. It's dark, I don't know where I am. I don't know which way to go. I feel so alone and helpless. I look up to the sky and stare at the moon and the stars. My grandmother's words are in my head when she says "God is everywhere. He's in the sun, he's in the moon…." I quietly ask God to help me. I don't want to die in the desert. I need strength and I need help to know which way to go. Finally, I start to calm down and think. The coyote had told me he walks with the moon to the right in the sky and then he knows he is going North. So, I get up, wipe off the dust and dirt on my clothes, drink some water and start walking.

As I am walking, I feel empty. There is a quiet nothingness that enters me every time I take a breath. It is so quiet. But I keep walking. I wish there was someone to guide me, to tell me what to do or which way to go, but I am completely alone and must depend on my own strength. I have to keep going. It's getting colder so I stop to put on my hoodie. I yell out again, "Help!", but it is useless. No one is there. I feel like I can't go on. But I have to, it's what I wanted. It feels like the end of the world, maybe it is. Maybe I will die somewhere in this desert and nobody will know who I am. I start talking to God. Why did you bring me this far to just die? I am trying to be a good person, I am trying to have a better life. Can't you help me? I keep walking. I start crying as I am walking.

I start thinking about how many people have died in the desert. How many people have died along the way to the border? How many people care that so many people have died? I have all these terrible thoughts. I try to –focus on my dreams to keep myself going, but my mind keeps going back to the nightmares. But I keep walking.

I don't know what time it is but I can see the sun is starting to come up in the sky. I still don't know where I am. It all looks the same. There's dirt and shrubs and nothingness. I decide to sit down and rest for a while. I drink some water. I have about half a gallon left. I've got to be careful and not run out of water. I pull out my sack and see that I don't have much food left. I am hungry but decide not to eat anything yet. I just sit and rest and close my eyes and pray to a God that I can't see and don't know if he is even listening to me.

After a while, I get up and I start walking again. With the sun coming up, the temperature is starting to go up and I take off my hoodie. I keep walking. My stomach starts to hurt because I am hungry. But I keep walking. My feet hurt, but I keep walking. My brain keeps telling me to keep walking. I walk for what feels like two or three hours. The sun is almost over my head and I remember the coyote said that is when we should stop to rest. So, I look for a place to hide in the shade from the sun. I see a big shrub up ahead and walk over to it. I take a few sips of my water and decide it's time to have one of my snacks. Then I take out my hoodie to use as a pillow and go to sleep.

I don't know how long I have slept. The sun is starting to go down in the sky. It is still very hot. I try to go back to sleep for a little more time but I can't turn off my brain. I need to stay calm, I need to think. I need to keep going. I won't quit. I will not die in this desert! I have come too far to die here!

The temperature starts dropping as the sun goes down. I know it's time to start walking again. I take a few more sips of my water. I am ready to start walking. There is no moon in the sky to figure out which way to go. I look around. I think. I try to remember which way I came from and then start walking again. I hope I'm going the right way. I don't want to go South. I keep talking to God and asking him to help me.

I am so glad the coyote told me to get good hiking boots. I have done a lot of walking. My legs hurt, my feet hurt, my back hurts, everything hurts yet I still feel numb inside. I walk for hours. The moon rises in the sky and I am going the right way! It is off to the right of me. I hear some coyotes howling in the distance. I hope they don't hear me walking. I keep walking. It's dark and I stumble over something on the ground. I look down and it is a skeleton. It makes me scared, but I get up and keep walking.

It's getting colder. I stop to put my hoodie on. How can the desert temperature change so much? In the daytime it feels like a furnace, in the night time it feels like a freezer. This is crazy! But I keep walking. I am so thirsty and decide to stop and take a few sips from the gallon of water. I am trying to be very careful that I don't run out, but I also don't want to die from dehydration. I sit for a while to rest my legs. I can do this. I am strong. I want a better life. Get up and keep walking.

I am losing track of time. I don't know what day it is, I don't know how long I have been in the desert. All I know is that I am tired, lonely and scared. But I keep walking. The sun is starting to come up in the distance so I know I must have walked for about ten hours. My legs are throbbing, my throat is dry. My stomach is yelling for food. But I keep walking.

It's getting hotter, so I stop to take off my hoodie. I take some more sips of my water. Now I have about a quarter of a gallon. The coyote told us that it would take 3 days to get across the desert. Has it been 3 days? Am I even going in the right direction? There are no signs. There's no one to ask. There's no GPS out in the wide, open desert.

I sit for a while and my stomach keeps yelling for food. I look in my sack and see that I have only 2 bags of chips left. If I eat one now, then I will be down to just one. There is no food out in the desert. I can't climb a tree and pick some fruit. I can't do work for the store owner to get some free food. What will I do if I run out of food? What will I do if I run out of water? I have to survive all of this!

I eat half a bag of chips. I let them sit in my mouth for a while and close my eyes and enjoy each bite. I have to keep enough food and water to survive. I have to make it. Ok, one more time I get up and start walking. I have to keep going until the sun is above my head and then I can rest. I can do this.

I start walking. It feels hotter today. It feels like my skin is starting to burn. It feels like my blood is beginning to boil. It feels like all my body parts are cooking inside me. My throat is filled with desert dirt. My lips are very dry and cracked. I think I am losing my mind. I don't know if I can make this. But I keep walking. Finally, the sun is over my head and I find a place to hide from the sun and sleep. I take a few more sips of water and lie down to sleep. I am so tired!

I wake up and it seems cooler. I am about to get up and notice that there is a rattlesnake coiled up next to my side sleeping. If I move, I will wake up the snake and he will bite me. I can't move until he slithers away. My heart is racing. I close my eyes and want to cry but there are no tears left. I have no water left inside my body. Please God, help me! I lay there for a long time and finally the snake starts moving away. I am safe. It is getting dark. I sit up and take some sips from my gallon jug. I decide to eat the rest of that bag of chips before I start walking again. I need energy to keep going.

By the time I am ready to walk I see the moon coming up in the sky so I know which way to go. I walk and I walk. I look around. I see the same dirt and shrubs everywhere in the darkness. I hope I am not walking around in circles. Every desert shrub looks the same….dry, wild and ugly. I start thinking about swimming with my friends back in Guatemala. That makes me thirsty. I have to think of other things. I start to think of America and all my hopes and dreams. That will help me stay strong and keep going. I keep walking.

I don't know how long I have been walking but I decide to take a rest. I take some more sips of my water. I am so thirsty but I only take 3 or 4 sips and then stop. I want to open up my last bag of chips, but I decide I will wait until I stop next time. My stomach is making funny noises but I have to be careful. I get up and keep walking.

It feels like the sun is starting to come up. I must have walked all night. I wonder how many miles I have walked. I wonder how close I am to the border. I know the coyote had told me that the city on the border was called Nogales. Am I getting closer? Am I going in the right direction? So many thoughts in my mind. But I keep walking.

My next break I take out the last bag of chips. I open it up and breathe in the smell. I have never smelled anything so good! I put one in my mouth and let it melt in my mouth. I am going to savor each bite. I have to make this food last. I eat about 5 or 6 chips and then put the rest back in my bag. I take 3 or 4 more sips of my water. I am getting down to the bottom of the gallon. I can't run out of water. I have to keep going. I get up and start walking again. I won't stop until the sun is over my head.

I have taken off my hoodie, as it is getting hot again. I keep walking. I think I see something in the distance, but my eyes may be playing tricks on me. I think I see some people. I start walking faster, even though my legs hurt. As I get closer there are people up ahead and there is some green. Maybe I am at the border. I start running.

I get closer and see about fifteen people sitting and standing around near a river. I walk over to them. They look surprised to see me. One man, the coyote, comes up to me and asks me where my group is. I tell him that I am all alone and that I have been walking for days in the desert. He can't believe I made it by myself. I sit down and start crying. The coyote brings me some water and tells me to drink slowly. He then gives me some food to eat. He asks if I have any money left and I told him that I don't. I gave it all to the coyote.

He says that I am getting very close to the border but that I must cross over the river. I look at it. It's very big and very deep. I know how to swim but the water is moving fast and I am so tired. He tells me that his group is resting up before they cross the river and that I can join them to cross but then I must go off by myself. He explains that they will all hold hands as they cross. The little ones will ride on the backs of the men and he will get everyone across. I think to myself that I am so tired that I don't think I am strong enough to cross, but if I don't go over with them then I may never make it. He tells me they will be leaving in about 30 minutes.

I go down to the river. I get in by the side to wash myself. It feels so good to be in water and cool down. I am so dirty. I am so thirsty. I am so hungry. I am so tired. I go back on land and lay down in the green grass. It feels good to be around people. I am so close. I made it through the desert, by myself. I can do this!

The coyote starts calling the group together. Everyone starts holding hands. There are about 8 men and the rest are women and children. I get in the middle of the hand chain. As we start to cross, I start to panic. I don't think I can do this. I am so tired. One of the men comes over to me and says "get on my back, I will carry you". I look at him. I don't know him but I am so tired that I just do it. He helps me across. God must have sent these people and that man to me. I don't know how I could have ever done this myself. I don't know how I survived in the desert as long as I did. I really think I am going to be able to do this.

We struggle to go across the river. In the middle of the river, it is moving very fast. But everyone holds hands and there is a lot of coaching and cheering as we make it across. When we get to the other side, I fall down on the ground and start crying again. I feel like a big baby, but I am so tired. The coyote comes over again and reminds me that I can't go on with them. He gives me a big new water bottle and some more food. He tells me a good place to go sleep for a while and rest. He tells me which way to walk when I feel stronger. He says I probably have about 3 or 4 more hours until I reach Arizona which is a state in the United States. I give him a hug and tell him thanks for everything. I shake the man's hand that helped me across the river. He pulls me in for a hug. I don't know these people but they are like God coming to help me. He does listen. He does hear our prayers.

I am so tired. It's time to go rest and sleep. I am still not there, but I am close. I have hope. I find a place to lay down. I pull out my hoodie out for a pillow and fall fast asleep. I sleep like a rock.

"We welcome refugees, not because they are American, but because, we are American."

Krish O'Mara Vigarajah, former refugee and now a public servant

More About Annunciation House

The weekend comes and goes. About 10 of the volunteers left and there is a fresh group coming in. I am now one of the "seasoned" volunteers even though I have only been here for less than a week. I am running the Travel Package Room and getting to know more about this place. There are so many parts that make up the whole and it runs like a well-oiled machine.

Each volunteer starts their shift by checking in at the Office. The Shift Volunteer Leader assigns jobs to everyone. I am always in the Travel Room. I usually am assigned one or two people to help with various tasks throughout our shift. We each are given a walkie talkie and must keep it with us at all times. It's our way of communicating inside this huge warehouse. We get messages about when Border Patrol is coming with a new busload of guests. We hear announcements about special needs and respond if they apply to us.

I continue my coordination of making peanut butter sandwiches and setting up travel bags for the outgoing guests. Every time a new busload comes, I pull out the Welcoming Cart to pass out bottles of water and snacks to the new arrivals. Often, I say "Bienvenidos" which means "welcome". I see a multitude of smiles but also some very tired, worn-out faces.

On one of the slower days, I ask to sit in on an intake interview with one of the volunteers. It is interesting to see how they take down the information about who is in the family, and where they are planning to go in the United States. An I phone is used to contact their Sponsor. As a guest is handed the phone to talk to their loved ones or whoever is helping them on the final part of their journey their eyes light up.

Some new questions have been added to the intake interview to find out more about the conditions of the detention centers. There have been reports of mistreatment and concerns about the length of stay that the Program Director wants to explore. One family that I am observing mentions they stayed at the Center for about a week. It took them about six weeks to travel from Honduras. They had a coyote who stayed with them. They rode buses and walked some. But because of their young children, they had to go slowly. They said some people stayed in the detention center a day or two and others stayed longer. This family was from Honduras and they weren't sure what countries the others were from that got processed quicker. The husband and wife were separated. The children went with their mother. But when it was time to be released, they were reunited.

Unfortunately, this is not always the case. We have had situations where the mother and children arrived at our facility while the father was still back at the detention center. When that happened, we would give them a longer stay hoping the family is reunited before moving on. But most guests only stay with us for two or three days before moving on.

Another unfortunate occurrence is that children who are eighteen years old or older were often separated from their parents because they are considered adults. I witnessed one case where the adult eighteen year old daughter was not sent at the same time as the rest of her family. The family grew very anxious when the daughter had not arrived by Day 2. That night at dinner a volunteer group had brought along fortune cookies for dessert. Many of the refugees couldn't understand the English messages inside so many of the volunteers went around and translated their messages. This family that was very anxious about their daughter got a fortune stating "what is lost will be found". And sure enough, their daughter showed up the next day on one of the Border Patrol buses. I heard and saw so many miracles like this throughout my stay.

When a sponsor is contacted it is their responsibility to arrange and pay for transportation to the chosen destination. Most guests are given bus tickets. A few receive airline tickets. Occasionally a Sponsor will drive down and pick people up. Whatever transportation is worked out gets communicated back to us with details of departure times and dates. I later learned that was what I was observing on my first day when people were answering the phones in the Office.

Once transportation is coordinated post-it notes on the office bulletin boards are moved from "Incoming" to "Outgoing". Outgoing notes now include transportation details. I had to check the Outgoing board three or four times a day to coordinate the travel packages for the outgoing guests.

Another team of volunteers managed "Maintenance". These volunteers were available for just about anything imaginable. For example, each morning after breakfast they would sweep and mop the Dormitorio, or sleeping area, and gather up any used bedding and towels from departing guests that would be taken to the Laundry Room. There was usually one person assigned to Laundry Services who kept the five commercial washers and dryers working all day long.

The Maintenance Crew would also pick up deliveries and see that they got to the right places. Sometimes there were Amazon orders coming from all around the country. Benefactors would send things like diapers, socks, and/or jars of peanut butter.

The Maintenance Crew also made sure all the port-a-potties had toilet paper and paper towels for hand washing. They cleaned the showers and restocked soap and shampoo in the dispensers. They emptied the trash in certain areas and brought it out to the dumpsters. And they were always around to fix anything they could when asked. These people didn't get the spotlight much, but their work was so important to keep everything running smoothly.

Annunciation House also had a Medical Clinic. There were several volunteer nurses there when I was working. They would see anyone after Intake that complained of any medical issues. The most common ailments were dehydration and headaches. But there were also cuts and wounds that needed to be treated and an occasional broken bone or sprained ankle. Pregnant women were checked to be sure everything was okay. More serious medical conditions were handled by On Call Doctors and sometimes people were transported to Emergency Departments. Several times during the week there were visiting Mobile Medical Vans that would come to provide care or service.

Finally, there was a Chapel that guests could visit any time of the day or night to pray. When there was a priest available, Masses were offered. I can't tell you how many times I walked past the Chapel and saw people in their praying or just giving thanks for their safe arrival.

"Remember, remember always, that the vast majority of us, and you and I especially, are descended from immigrants."

President Franklin D. Roosevelt

Pedro

Arrival to the United States!

I wake up and look around. I have no idea what time it is. The sun is past being over my head. I think I slept a full day! It is still really hot and I decide to rest some more and let the sun start to go down a little so it won't be so hot. My body is tired, but my spirit is excited because I know I am getting close. The coyote told me which direction to walk and what I may see along the way. He said I may get to the U.S. in a few more hours.

I drink some of the water the coyote gave me and eat some of the food. I want to have energy for the next part of my journey. The sun is starting to go lower in the sky. Even though it is still hot, I am too excited to wait so I start walking.

My legs and feet still hurt but I get a good pace going and keep looking around for other people or animals. All I see are the mountains ahead of me and big open spaces where the desert is starting to become more green. There are more trees and plants growing as I walk and I see a few desert flowers. This makes me more happy that I am getting out of the hot desert.

Up ahead I see a fence. The coyote told me there would be fences along the way made out of wire and I should be careful when I crawl under them so I don't catch my clothes on the Xs. He said it is called barbed wire. He told me the farmers in the United States use these fences to keep their animals inside. I still don't see any animals. I see lots of open space with grass.

I get closer to the mountains and shake my head thinking that I have one more problem to face. It is hard to walk up the mountain but I go sideways and take my time. It is good that I am young. It is good that I am healthy. I can stop and rest if I need to. I climb the mountain and keep looking down to see how far I have walked up and look out to see how far I have come since the desert. It is beautiful to look out. Far away I see some animals. I think they are cows. I keep climbing the mountain.

I would say it took me about three hours to get to the top. I don't have a watch. My phone needs to be charged. I just know the sun is going lower in the sky. I look on the other side of the mountain and see almost all green. There is no more desert. I am so happy that I don't have to do that again!

I start going down the other side of the mountain. It is much easier to go down than up. It is starting to get darker and cooler. When I get near the bottom of the mountain there is another wire fence. I crawl under and then keep walking. I can hear coyotes howling in the distance. It's getting cooler so I put on my hoodie. Am I in the U.S. now? There is no sign that says, "Welcome". So, I just keep walking.

As I walk, I start thinking about my dreams of a better life. I want to learn English. I want to go to school. I want to get a job. And I want to save my money to get a nice house. I want to find a good wife and start a family when I am older. I want to be happy. These thoughts help me to keep going.

Up ahead I see some big animals. They are bigger than cows. I think they are buffalo but there is no one to ask. I walk away from them because I don't know if they are friendly or not. They are eating grass and don't bother me. I come to another wire fence and crawl under it.

I see the moon coming up in the sky and I keep it on my right side. That way I know that I am going in the right direction. I keep walking and

I think I hear something up ahead. It sounds like voices. I start walking a little faster and I think I see a group of people walking. I get close to them and they look like me. They look Spanish. I ask them if we are in the U.S.? One tells me "not yet, but we are close."

I ask them if I can walk with them and they say "ok". I don't understand everything they are saying, but I understand some. It's nice to be around people again. It makes me more happy. We walk for about another hour and then up ahead we see a big wall fence. Some people have told me there is a big wall on the border to keep people out. But it won't stop me.

As we get closer, we start talking about how we will get over this wall. We all work together. They ask me if I am brave and I laugh. I tell them that I walked through the desert by myself and I have been traveling alone for almost a week. Then one of the men asked me if I will go up first to the top of the wall and help them get over. I say "sure, if you help me get up to the top." So, one man puts his two hands together and I put my foot in and he lifts me up. Two other men help me get higher and I reach the top. I sit on the wall and try to balance. Another young man about my age comes up to the top and sits across from me facing me. Then slowly the others are lifted up to us and we help them get to the top and go over. They have to jump down because we stay on the top until everyone has made it over. When everyone is over, we all cheer and give high fives to each other.

We think now we are in the United States. But there are no signs, so we are not sure. They want to stay and rest. I want to keep going so I leave most of them behind. A couple of young men join me and we keep walking. One is from Honduras, the other is from El Salvador. We walk for about an hour and then stop to rest and have some food and water.

As we are getting up from our rest to continue walking a car pulls up to us on the dirt road. It is the police. We start to run but the police yell to stop running. I stop because I was told that once in the U.S. the police will help me. The other two run away. The policeman speaks to me in English, but I don't understand. Then he speaks to me in Spanish and I only understand a little of what he says. He asks how old I am and I tell him that I am 15. I put my hands out to be handcuffed and he shakes his head and just escorts me to the police car. I get in the back seat and he drives me to the police station.

There is another police officer there that speaks better Spanish but I still don't understand everything he is saying to me. He is asking me questions but I shake my head because I don't know what he is saying. He picks up the phone and calls a number and then puts it on speaker phone and there is a woman who speaks a Spanish that I can understand. I start answering the questions.

I learn that I am in the city of Tucson, Arizona. The woman asks for a phone number of someone to call back in Guatemala and I tell her that I have nobody to call. She asks me lots of questions about where I came from and how I got where I was and why I came to the U.S. I try to answer but I am also scared. She tells me that I will stay in the jail there for one night and then the police will take me to a city named Phoenix where I will live with other young people and get some help from them.

The police put me in a jail cell all by myself and give me some food and water to drink. I am scared, but they seem to be nice so I finally fall asleep on a nice soft bed. I wake up and it is morning. The same policeman that picked me up comes and tells me to come with him. We get in a car and he starts driving me to this new city. We don't talk because I can't understand him and he can't understand me. The lady told me I would like the place I was going and I hoped that she was telling me the truth. I was in the car for about two hours and I kept looking out at all the new places we passed. I couldn't believe I was finally in the United States!

We pulled up to a big brick building with a large fence around it. I could see a lot of young people outside. Some were sitting, some were playing soccer, some were playing basketball. I smiled and thought I was going to be okay now. The policeman brought me inside and then he left.

I met with a new woman who asked me many of the same questions I was asked in Tucson. She kept asking me if I wanted to call anyone back home and I told her that there was no one to call. She took me to another room and told me I could take a shower and pick out some new clothes. Then I went to a smaller part of the building and met some more people. Some of them spoke Spanish that I could understand, others I only understood parts of what they said. I was told that I would be living in an area with twelve other boys my age.

At my new "home" we were each given a space that was ours and told to keep it clean. We were also assigned various jobs to do. The food here was good. I would go to school for part of the day to learn English and Spanish and about the U.S. and how people live here. The rest of the day was free time to relax, talk with friends or play. All of this made me very happy.

I met lots of other boys and some girls from Guatemala. There were also teens from Honduras, El Salvador, Nicaragua, Ecuador and Peru. Most of them were like me. Everyone was under eighteen years old and came into the country without family. We were called "unaccompanied minors". The staff seemed nice and told me that they would look for a place for me to go and be sponsored. I didn't really understand. But after about eight months they came and told me that I was being sponsored by Catholic Family Services in Rochester, New York and would be living in a foster home and going to high school. This made me happy.

"It says something about our country that people around the world are willing to leave their homes and leave their families and risk everything to come to America. Their talent and hard work and love of freedom have helped make America the leader of the world. And our generation will ensure that America remains a beacon of liberty and the most hope filled society this world has ever known."

President George W. Bush

Judy

More Stories and Experiences from Annunciation House

I had less contact with the guests while working in the Travel Packaging Room but I was able to interact with them during mealtimes. I also heard a lot of stories from fellow volunteers who conducted the incoming interviews and who had their own interactions with the guests. Every story is different, but there are some striking similarities. The guests often describe increased violence in their hometowns and a search for a better life. Not necessarily the American Dream, but where they feel safe and not afraid of being killed. Here are a few of the more memorable stories…

One day at lunch I sat with a mother and her two teenage children, a boy and girl. I asked them where they had come from and they told me southern Mexico. It took them two weeks to travel North and the girl mentioned that her father had been killed by the local Gang. She started getting teary eyed. Her mother continued the story stating the Gang was trying to recruit her son to work with them. Her husband had stepped in to prevent this and he was killed by them. She decided it wasn't safe to stay where they were and they took as much as they could carry and left the next morning. They came through the port of entry and passed the Credible Fear Interview, as all others at Annunciation House had done. The son told me they had stayed about 10 days in the detention center waiting to move on to Chicago. They were finally released and sent to us at Annunciation House.

I asked who lived in Chicago and they told me it was their father's brother who was sponsoring them. I told them I was from New York and that we had similar weather. I took out my I phone and showed them a picture of me playing with my grandchildren in some snow drifts. Their eyes widened and I told them that starting in November or December the temperature would be dropping and the snow would come and stay until about March or April. I think I may have scared them a little, but I wanted to prepare them for the different climate they would be living in.

I saw the two teens later in the playroom and I had some time to sit with them and teach them some common English phrases like "I don't understand," and "Can you please repeat that again slower?" I wrote these phrases in both English and Spanish and told them to practice on the bus ride to Chicago. Their mother came up to me as they were leaving the next day and asked if she could take a picture of me with her family. I often think about this family and hope they are doing well in their new home.

I remember another meal visit with several young mothers and their toddlers. One mother was from El Salvador and she told me how she and about three other families were locked in an office-like room in the detention center. She said there was a tiny window to look out. They were allowed out three to four times a day to use the restroom. Her eighteen month old son was potty training and she knocked on the door to ask if she could bring her son to the bathroom but was told "no", it wasn't their time yet. Her son was unable to hold it and wet his pants and she didn't have any other clothes to change him into. She was so grateful that they were given gently used clothes in this place and she could wash his pants and hang them to dry. Several of the other mothers were nodding while she was telling her story. They talked about how cold the detention centers were and that they were only given frozen burritos once a day to eat. They were all so grateful we were treating them with respect and dignity here.

Some men described being separated from their wives and children in the detention centers. They were often put in crowded areas, sometimes having to take turns standing, sitting, or lying down to sleep. There was a toilet in the center of the room that they all had to use with no privacy. This was all happening in the United States of America! How can we treat people like this?

Several times we heard stories about how people had paid coyotes to help them get to the border. Some were good, but several reported the coyotes took their money and abandoned them along the way. There were also people that had been kidnapped and held until the ransom was paid. These people had to contact family or friends to try to get money to pay the kidnappers. If they didn't get the money the people were tortured or killed. One family reported this had happened to them. They had left their home in May and were just now arriving to our facility in October. They lost over $10,000 with an abandoned coyote, a kidnapping, and other unexpected expenses along the way.

Another family from Mexico told me the reason they left their village was that every week the Drug Cartel came to their home to collect money. At first it was about half of the father's weekly income, but it kept increasing. He said they didn't have enough money left to pay the bills and survive anymore. He said he asked the police for help but they did nothing and were corrupt.

One mother reported at intake that she came North because her two sons were reaching puberty and that is the time that the Gangs start recruiting them. She wanted to keep them safe. When she got to the border, she had to wait to enter the U.S. A police officer helped them to find a place to stay while they waited for their number to come up to enter the country. They lived at a local nursing home and she cooked and cleaned in exchange for a room for her family. She then asked her two sons to leave the interview and she reported that the staff at the nursing home were raping her every day. She didn't want her sons to hear that, and she was now so grateful to be in a safe country and to give them a better life.

There was a young disabled boy who came through with his mother. I believe he may have been autistic. They were given a separate room in the dorm area where the staff slept to get away from all the noise and distractions. I brought them some coloring books and crayons, a stuffed animal and a few Spanish picture books. We brought them their meals and the mother seemed so appreciative of the quiet place and special care that we provided.

Sometimes at the end of my shift I would go into the playroom for an hour to be with the children. There is nothing like watching young, innocent children laugh and play. I sat with one mother one day and she said she and her family had lived by the bridge at the port of entry for three weeks while waiting to be called to enter the U.S. Then they spent two weeks in a detention center and now they are finally in the U.S. She said with tears in her eyes that she didn't think that this day would ever come when her kids could move around and play again. She was most grateful.

On my last full day, I met a young pregnant mother with two young children at lunch. She had traveled from Honduras and looked totally exhausted. I remarked it must be very difficult traveling alone with two young children. She told me she had started out with her parents and two younger sisters. I asked where they were. She said her parents had been killed along the way. Her two younger sisters were still back at the detention center. They had been separated from her since she was not their parent. They were only ten and thirteen years old. My Spanish was getting pretty good by the end of the month, but I wanted to be sure that I had understood correctly what she told me. I called the Shift Coordinator over and told her quickly what I had understood and asked if she could verify this. She did and immediately went to the office to call Ruben Garcia, the Head of Annunciation House. They began the process of trying to reunite this family. I never heard the final result, but I am hopeful that they were able to bring this family back together. They had been through enough!

I am not sure what is happening to those who were not granted asylum to enter the country. Some of the volunteers went into Juarez, Mexico on their days off and described the thousands of migrants lined up along the fence. Some had tents, others had old cardboard boxes they were being used for shelter. They were camping out on the streets, waiting for another chance to enter the country. Near the end of October, I know the temperature was dropping down into the 30s at night and I often thought about those people when I made my nightly visit to the port-o-potty. I had to bundle up for my quick trip to the bathroom. How were they surviving out on the street?

I worked the morning shifts but often I went back in the evening for some of the activities offered by the volunteers. One evening there was a Pinata Party in El Dormitorio. They celebrated all the birthdays of children from that month and there was music playing and some dancing. It brought a lot of smiles and laughter to everyone and a feeling of normalcy.

Another late afternoon we set up a nail salon for the young girls and mothers. They could select their favorite color and get a manicure. There were often pick up soccer or kickball games going on with anyone that wanted to play.

It has been four years since I volunteered at Annunciation House but these stories and experiences will stay with me forever.

"Illegal immigration is not a new problem. Native Americans used to call it "white people."

Unknown

Pedro

Moving to Rochester, NY

I was told that I would be moving to Rochester, NY. I had no idea where that was and the staff showed me a map and explained that it was up north near Canada. They also told me the temperature was very different from what I was used to. I saw some pictures of snow and just smiled thinking that it looked beautiful and this would be a new adventure for me. I had mixed feelings about the move. I had made many friends at the detention center but I also knew that I hadn't come to the U.S. to live in this place. I was ready to start the next part of my journey. So, after packing up all my things and saying my goodbyes, I was taken to the airport.

I couldn't believe how far I could travel in one day on an airplane. It was my first time flying and a staff member from the detention center came with me. That was good because I had no idea what would happen, and she explained it all to me along the way. On the airplane I sat by the window and looked down to see the land below and the fluffy clouds that were above. It was unbelievable! I wasn't scared but it was like nothing I could have ever imagined. My heart was racing when we finally landed.

There were two people waiting for us when we got off the plane. One was my new Case Manager from Catholic Family Services and the other was my foster mother. I smiled at them but didn't say much. My foster mother didn't speak Spanish. She talked slowly, but I didn't really understand too much of what she was saying. The Case Manager spoke Spanish but it sounded different from the Spanish I had heard down at the detention center or in Guatemala. I understood much more of what she said to me.

She welcomed me to Rochester and told me how happy they were to have me come to live in this city. I said goodbye to the staff person that had escorted me and who was going to return to Phoenix on another flight.

I arrived in Rochester in January 2018. Nobody could have explained to me how cold I would feel when I went outside. There was no snow on the ground but it was very cold and windy. My hands and face were freezing! We all got into a car and went to my new home. I was tired, but also excited about starting the next part of my life. The Case Manager said I would get $600 to buy clothes and she said it was important that I got a warm coat, gloves and a hat. I couldn't believe I was getting all of this for free. I asked if I had to pay it back and she said it is part of the foster care system.

I settled into my new home. I was living in the city of Rochester in a big house and I had my own bedroom. This was quite different from where I had been living for the past nine months. There were no other children and my foster mother was older and we had a hard time communicating. It was very hard for me. The next week it snowed and there was about a foot of snow on the ground. I was so cold when I went outside, even while wearing my new winter coat, hat and gloves. I couldn't believe people could live in this weather.

I started school right away and was put in the ninth grade at the Rochester International Academy. This school had people from all around the world who were like me learning English and adjusting to a new culture. I met a lot of Spanish speakers and it felt good to be around young people. But the classes I went to were very, very hard! I liked the English classes but all the other classes were too hard for me. Sometimes I would ask to go to the bathroom in the middle of class and I wouldn't go back until the bell rang. When the weather got nicer outside, I would get off the bus and walk away from the school and just walk around the city until it was time to get on the bus to go back home.

When I got home from school, my foster mother was not there. She was still at work. She seemed to go out a lot at night and I was often at home alone. I felt very lonely and often went to my bedroom and cried. I felt like the world was falling down on me. I got sick a lot when I first moved to Rochester. I don't know if it was from the cold or from being around new diseases. I was very sad and wondered if I had made the right decision to come to the U.S. I didn't expect it would be this hard. In quiet times, the flashbacks came back more often to haunt me. I also started having nightmares about my travels and I was afraid to fall back asleep sometimes.

Every month I was given $40.00 from Catholic Family Services. I saved the money and when I had $120, I called my uncle to find out where my friend Cesar was. I remembered my promise to him and I wanted to send him money so that he could come join me in the U.S. My uncle told me that Cesar had been shot dead for stealing food. This made me feel so sad and guilty for having left him behind.

My Case Worker would come to the house to meet with me and ask me how things were going. I didn't want to tell her too much because I was scared she would send me back. But she could tell I had a lot of sadness and strong feelings about everything I had lived through. She told me the school was sending her reports and she asked me why I was skipping school. I told her I was having a really hard time and she said she'd like me to go to see a Counselor to help me with my feelings. At first, I didn't want to go, but she told me to try it out and it would probably help.

I started seeing the Counselor after school and she helped me to talk about what had happened to me. She kept telling me that I was safe now and would have a better life. I told her about my nightmares and trouble sleeping. I asked her how to forget all the bad stuff and she said I should bury it all in the ground and cover it with dirt. She told me I can start a new life here in the U.S. and I can make whatever I want from life. She helped me a lot and I started feeling better.

Once a month, Catholic Family Services would have a group meeting with other kids like me and I really enjoyed going to these events. I met some other people from Honduras, Guatemala and Central American countries. We all talked and laughed and shared our stories with each other.

I met one boy a year older than me named Juan and he seemed really nice. He was living alone in a foster home out in a suburb and he too felt lonely. We got talking at these meetings and wished that we could be together. After a few months, the Case Manager told me that I would be moving to live in the same foster home as Juan. I was so happy because now I wouldn't be alone. I moved to the Juan's foster home in July 2019.

I liked the new school. There were not as many students like me there, but the teachers were all very friendly and helped me a lot. I also started speaking more English because there were not as many Spanish speakers there. I only missed one day of school my first year and that was because I had to go to immigration court. I think it also helped to have my friend, Juan, who was like my brother.

Even though I liked the new school, I didn't like living so far away from the city. There wasn't a lot to do after school or on the weekends. Often, I would get on my bike and ride around and eventually end up in the city. I missed the freedom of going places when I wanted I did not like sitting at home all the time. I met another young man from Honduras at the Catholic Family group meetings and he lived in another foster home in the city. We became good friends and I told my Case Manager I would like to move back into the city and asked if I could stay at my new friend's house. After a few months a bed opened up there and I was able to move there. Now that I was in the city again, I had more freedom to go out and do things. When my friend, Juan, graduated from high school he also moved to this foster home and the three of us became like brothers.

COVID hit in 2020 and I had to do a lot of schoolwork on computers. That was hard, but the teachers helped us a lot. The NY state exams were canceled and as long as I did the schoolwork, I passed all my classes. I was able to graduate in 2021.

After graduation I got a job at a local mini mart store. I was nineteen years old and it felt good to be earning my own money. They had me put food and drinks into the walk-in coolers and it was very cold. I did this job for about three days and then told them that I didn't really like this job so I quit. I tried working in a restaurant but didn't like that kind of work either. I then got a job in construction. I learned how to do roofing. I liked working with my hands, but the job was really hot in the summer months. But this job only lasted until November when it got cold and the roofing business slowed down. I stayed at home for a few months and tried to figure out what I could do.

I went back to the mini mart near my home and asked if I could come back and work as a store clerk. The boss said he would try me out to see if I could do it and I have been working at that place now for the past two years. I feel so good to be earning my own money and getting more and more independent. When I turned 21, the Case Manager told me that now it was time to move out of the foster care system and into my own place.

"We are not all in the same boat. We are in the same storm. Some have super yachts. Some have canoes with just one oar. Some are drowning. Just be kind and help whoever you can."

Damian Barr, writer

Judy

Annunciation House Stories of Generosity

One of the things that truly amazed me about my month long stay at this place was the generosity of strangers. I had mentioned earlier that El Paso Transit Bus Service provided one or two bus trips each day to the local Greyhound station and the airport. The Red Cross provided 1000 cots and blankets for use in El Dormitorio. Several local churches and organizations provided meals and serving and cleaning up on a weekly or monthly basis. And there were El Paso Community members that volunteered on a weekly basis. A religious nun came in at lunchtime a couple of times a week with her ukulele and she would walk around the cafeteria singing. Most of the songs were in Spanish but sometimes she would add an English song or two. This brought smiles to everyone's faces. On Saturdays, there were usually three or four military cadets that came to volunteer and were assigned to my area for special projects.

In addition, there were donations made by local and some national organizations, businesses and foundations. Being in the Travel Room I saw large shipments of peanut butter, water bottles, snack foods arriving, as well as diapers. There were Amazon deliveries of socks, underwear and other items that came through from all over the country. It was amazing and uplifting to see the generosity of people nearby and from a distance. To me this just reinforced the concept that there is still a lot of goodness in our society.

As I was preparing for my trip, I went on the Annunciation House website and read about how the Detention Centers were releasing huge amounts of migrants to the streets back in December 2018. When that happened Annunciation House started working closely with some local hotels to provide rooms for some of these families. I watched a video how one woman described working at the front desk on Christmas Eve called her husband at home and told him to call several of their church friends to go to Walmart or Dollar stores to buy up as many coloring books, stuffed animals and toys as they could for the children, wrap them and bring them to the hotel. She wanted to be sure that these children had something to unwrap on Christmas morning. That story brought tears to my eyes. And it reminded me of the Christmas Story of "no room at the inn". But this "inn" was providing room and much more!

The volunteers themselves donate their time but also pay for all of their travel expenses to get to the facility. Some stay in local hotels, but most live in the communal setting like I did. A few rented cars and offered to drive guests to the airports and help them check in.

Several volunteers brought money collected from their hometowns or local churches or organizations when they came. I had a few friends who gave me money and asked me to see that it was put to good use while I was there. And I know that my church took up a collection and sent in money while I was there. Also, from my daily Facebook posts there were some donations made.

People from all over the country have also provided financial assistance to Annunciation House. I was genuinely touched when one of the guests who had stayed with us for three days came into the office on her last day and handed us $5.00. She said that she had $10.00 left to her name, but she wanted to offer a donation so that others could be helped as she had. That reminded me of the Bible story of the poor woman who puts two coins into the temple collection in thanksgiving and gratefulness. We tried to give it back to her to use for her travel to her Sponsor, but she was adamant, so we kept it.

So, if you are reading this book and feel so inclined to make a financial donation to Annunciation House, you can visit their website to review the options for online payment. Or you can send a check made out to "Annunciation House" and send to P.O. Box 11190, El Paso, Texas 79995-1189. They are a non-profit organization and all donations are tax deductible. Money donations, both large and small will definitely be appreciated and put to good use.

"Sometimes the strength within you is not a big fiery flame for all to see, it's just a tiny spark that whispers softly, "you've got this, keep going."

Unknown

Pedro

My Final Thoughts

I moved into my first apartment in July 2023 with Juan, one of my foster brothers that I have known since living in Rochester. We didn't have a lot of personal possessions, mostly clothes, bedding and a few keepsakes. But we were both proud and happy to be independent living in our first home.

Juan's former teacher and my new friend helped us by finding this apartment near where I work. She explained how a lease works and how to hook up the electricity. She also got a lot of things for the apartment from her own home and some of her friends. It's hard to accept all this kindness from people I don't even know, but she explained that there are a lot of good people in this country who want to help us to get started. I am truly grateful.

The first night in my apartment, I sat with my friend/brother and we talked about our lives and how far we have come. I thought back to when I was in the desert, all alone and thinking I might die, I never imagined having a full time job and my own place to live at age 21. I am so close to having my green card and permanent residence.

Suddenly it hits me, everything….all those days and nights of desperation, walking in the desert, running for my life…all the nights of crying and fearing and starving. All those times I wanted to give up. It all really happened. All of it. To me. It's finally over. I have made it!

I am definitely not rich, but I have all that I need for now. I have more dreams I want to accomplish. I want to save up for a car and someday a house. I hope to be married by the age of 30 and start my own family. I hope I will do better as a father than my own.

When I started to retell my story for this book, I had to unbury many of the memories. I may have gotten some of the events or times mixed up, but they all happened. Surprisingly, the nightmares didn't come back. In fact, while I was being interviewed, I realized how strong I was and still am. I did all of this as a kid. I survived on my own and lived through so many obstacles. All of that made me stronger and now I appreciate so much of life.

I wanted to tell my story so that others would know what I went through. I wanted people to understand why so many are trying to come to this country. This is a place of so many opportunities and the possibility to have a better life. I wanted to tell this story for all of those people who didn't make it or couldn't tell their stories.

"I'd rather live next door to someone who crossed a desert to become an American than an American who wouldn't cross the street to help a stranger."

Human Reform Politics (Facebook post)

Judy

My Final Thoughts

My life and perspective have been forever changed from this volunteer experience. I no longer take for granted all the blessings in my life. We are so lucky to be able to walk up to a water fountain or a faucet to get fresh water. We have flushing toilets and toilet paper. Hot showers, soap, shoes, a change of clothes, heat or air conditioning are luxuries that many people don't have.

My month long stay at the border ended but the thoughts and memories of my time there have stayed with me. I was a witness to a shattered world as some guests shared their harrowing journeys and the horrific circumstances of their lives. Many families had not eaten for days. The children and adults were scared, scarred, and traumatized. I saw the children change right before my eyes as they realized they were now safe as they saw their parents relax and begin smiling again.

I have tried to capture some of the moments I experienced and describe what I saw, heard and witnessed from people. I am glad that I have been able to write this and hope that by reading it you have learned something more about what is happening at the border. I don't really know what the answer may be to the immigration crisis in our country, but I do know that because many innocent human beings who are simply trying to find a better life are involved, the situation deserves to be addressed.

I am a U.S. citizen. I was lucky to be born in this country and have always enjoyed the freedom and safety of living here. I hope never to take for granted these privileges and blessings. But with these privileges, I feel obligated to do more for those that were not awarded the same.

None of us choose the life and circumstances we are born into. But we can choose how we deal with them. For those with privilege, we can choose to live a life focused on our own needs, or we can choose to help those of different circumstances.

Many people may feel the same as me and wonder what they can do? You do not need to go down to the border. Every town or city in this country has people in need. It may be the homeless, the veterans, or maybe a refugee family that has just moved into your neighborhood. Volunteer opportunities are out there. Make a monetary donation. Make a Good Will donation of clothing, household items or furniture. Provide one to one literacy class. Vote for legislators who will address the immigration issues.

If you discover a refugee family has moved into your neighborhood, stop in and introduce yourself. Make them feel welcome. Maybe bring a tray of cookies. Offer to drive them to appointments or for errands. Answer questions they may have, help them read and sort their mail. Sometimes It's hard to know what is important and what is junk. Take them shopping and show them where the discount and thrift shops are.

If you are part of a school, church, business or organization you might suggest running a food or clothing drive for a local refugee center, homeless shelter or soup kitchen. Instead of exchanging gifts with families and/or friends who have everything, make purchases for these places or give a donation in their name. Share these stories or this book with a friend.

There are still thousands of stories like Pedro's that we will never hear or read about. But maybe the next time you see a news clip about the southern border, perhaps you will remember some of Pedro's story and the stories from the people I encountered in El Paso.

We may not all look the same or speak the same language. But we all live under the same sun and stars, drink the same water and breathe the same air. We are united as one human race and should all be treated with human kindness, respect and dignity.

"The world will not be destroyed by those who do evil, but by those who watch them without doing anything."

Albert Einstein

DISCUSSION QUESTIONS

If you had to flee your home today, alone or with your family, and could only pack one backpack, what would you take?

If your family was relocating to China, what do you think would be the biggest challenge?

What are some of the differences in travel between Judy and Pedro?

What parts of the book really stood out to you?

Which quote at the beginning of each chapter did you like and why?

How has this book changed your perspective?

What are you grateful for in your life?

Acknowledgments

A special thank you to Pedro who was brave enough to tell his story. He had to relive some memories that he had buried. But he wanted other to know his story. I hope I did him justice.

And I'd like to personally thank my friend, Dorothy Schwind and my brother, Paul Predmore for editing my first draft. And I thank all of those who encouraged me to write about my experiences from Annunciation House.